The Owl
and the
Pussy-cat

by Edward Lear

illustrated by Gwen Fulton

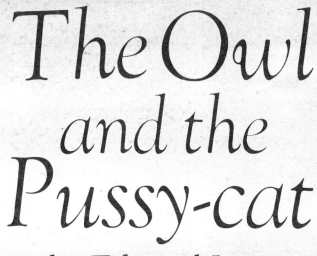

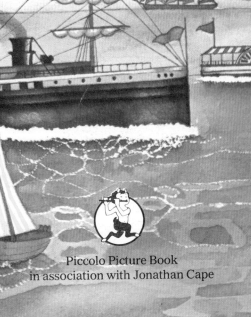

Piccolo Picture Book
in association with Jonathan Cape

The Owl and the Pussy-cat
went to sea
In a beautiful pea-green boat,

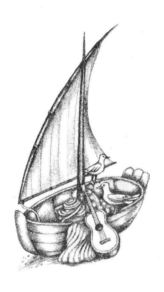

They took some honey,
     and plenty of money,
Wrapped up in a five-pound note.

The Owl looked up
        to the stars above,
And sang to a small guitar,
"O lovely Pussy! O Pussy, my love,
What a beautiful Pussy you are,
        You are,
        You are!
What a beautiful Pussy you are!"

Pussy said to the Owl,
     "You elegant fowl!
How charmingly sweet you sing!
O let us be married!
     too long we have tarried:
But what shall we do for
     a ring?"

They sailed away,
   for a year and a day,
To the land
   where the Bong-tree grows.

And there in a wood
     a Piggy-wig stood
With a ring at the end of his nose,
     His nose,
     His nose,
With a ring at the end of his nose.

"Dear Pig, are you willing
        to sell for one shilling
                Your ring?"
Said the Piggy,
                "I will."

So they took it away,
     and were married next day
By the Turkey who lives
          on the hill.

They dined on mince,
     and slices of quince
Which they ate
     with a runcible spoon;

And hand in hand,
        on the edge of the sand,
They danced by the light of the moon,
        The moon,
        The moon,
They danced by the light of the moon.

First published 1977 by Jonathan Cape Ltd
This Piccolo edition published 1980 by
Pan Books Ltd,
Cavaye Place, London SW10 9PG
In association with Jonathan Cape
9 8
Illustrations © Gwen Fulton 1977
ISBN 0330 26101 0
Printed in England by
Michael Stephen Press